PEANUT BUTTER

At a peanut butter factory, special machines remove the skins from peanuts before they are ground.

PEANUT BUTTER

Arlene Erlbach

Lerner Publications Company • Minneapolis

Dedicated to my father, Morris Faverman, who was born near the Peanut City—A. E.

Illustrations by Jackie Urbanovic

Words printed in **bold** are explained in the glossary on page 44.

Text copyright © 1994 by Arlene Erlbach
Illustrations copyright © 1994 by Lerner Publications Company

Library of Congress Cataloging-in-Publication Data

Erlbach, Arlene.
   Peanut butter/by Arlene Erlbach.
     p. cm.—(How it's made)
   Includes index.
   Summary: Describes how peanut butter is made, from the cultivation of the peanuts through filling the jars with the nutty spread. Includes simple, no-bake recipes.
    ISBN 0-8225-2387-6
    1. Peanut butter—juvenile literature. [1. Peanut butter. 2. Peanuts.]
I. Title.
II. Series: Erlbach, Arlene. How it's made.
TP438.P4E75 1994   93–20217
641.3'56596—dc20   CIP
                          AC

Manufactured in the United States of America
1 2 3 4 5 6 – I/JR – 99 98 97 96 95 94

CONTENTS

In the United States, more people eat peanut butter than any other food item.

America's Most Popular Spread

What tastes delicious between two slices of bread? What's even better with bananas or jelly? More than 20 million kids eat it every day. Can you guess what it is? You're right—it's peanut butter.

No other American food is as popular as peanut butter. Every second, somebody in the United States or Canada buys a jar. About 800 million pounds of peanut butter are eaten each year. Do you know how much peanutty spread that is? That's enough for everybody in the United States and Canada to make 84 peanut butter sandwiches.

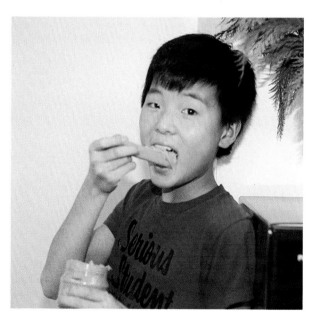

- Peanut butter was invented more than 100 years ago. We celebrated its 100th birthday in 1990.

- Peanut butter was originally invented by a doctor. He created it for his patients who needed a form of protein that was easy to chew and to digest.

Peanut butter is usually made from crushed peanuts, salt, vegetable oil, and a sweetener. A 12-ounce jar contains about 520 peanuts. The 18-ounce size contains 810. According to a law made by the United States government, at least 90 percent of the ingredients must be peanuts. Otherwise, a manufacturer cannot call its product peanut butter.

Lots of things happen to peanuts before they end up in a jar at the store. They have to be grown, picked, shelled, roasted, crushed, and mixed with the other ingredients. Many people in many different jobs do these things to bring the peanut butter to you. People who take part in making and selling a product are part of its industry.

Kids are an important part of the peanut butter industry. When you eat peanut butter, you are a consumer, or end user, of the product.

Ninety-nine percent of American families with children have a jar of peanut butter in their refrigerator or on the kitchen shelf. More than half of all peanut butter sold is consumed by kids. By the time you graduate from high school, you'll probably have eaten about 1,500 peanut butter sandwiches. Without you, the peanut butter industry wouldn't be as big as it is.

Want to know more about an industry in which *you* play an important part? Smear some peanut butter on a cracker or a slice of bread. Take a bite and turn the page.

Most U.S. peanut farms are located in Georgia, Alabama, North Carolina, Texas, Oklahoma, Virginia, and Florida. These states have the warm climate and sandy soil that peanuts need to grow.

2

Not Nuts At All

The main ingredient of peanut butter—the peanut—isn't really a nut. Peanuts are actually vegetables, like peas or beans. Peanuts are seeds of the peanut plant.

When peanut seeds are planted, they grow into bushes about 18 inches high. Delicate yellow flowers appear on the stems. When the petals fall off, they leave behind buds called pegs. The stems with pegs on them drop to the ground and enter the soil, where they grow into peanuts. So peanuts aren't picked from the peanut bushes. They grow underground, and farmers dig them up.

Thirty to forty days after the seeds are planted, the peanut plants bloom.

When the peanuts are ready to be dug up, farmers harvest them with machines called diggers and shakers. A digger and a shaker are attached to a tractor. The digger is a long blade that digs into the ground. It loosens the peanut plant from the soil and cuts off the root. The shaker lifts the plant from the soil and shakes off the dirt and sand. Then the shaker lays the plant on the ground with the peanuts facing up.

With a digger and a shaker, a farmer pulls row after row of peanut plants from the soil.

Peanuts are left in the field for several days so that they can dry in the sun.

Freshly dug peanuts don't look very much like the crisp tan nuts you shell and eat. They don't look appetizing at all. They still have leaves and stems on them, and they're muddy and wet. The farmer leaves the peanuts in the field for a few days so they can dry in the sun. Peanuts must be dried or they will spoil before they become peanut butter or any other peanut product.

- An African word for peanut is *nguba*. "Goober," the slang word for peanut, comes from this word.
- The United States produces 4 billion pounds of peanuts a year. Half of those peanuts are used to make peanut butter.

When the peanuts are dry, the farmer rides through the field on a combine—a harvesting machine that collects and cleans crops. The combine picks up the peanut plants and places them into a box called a hopper. Then the combine separates the leaves and stems from the peanuts. The peanuts stay inside the hopper, and the leaves and stems are thrown back onto the field. The leaves and stems won't go to waste, though. The farmer may use them later to fertilize the peanut field or to feed to cows and pigs.

A farmer harvests the peanut crop with a machine called a combine.

From the combine hopper, the peanuts are dumped into drying trailers. There, hot air circulates around the peanuts until they are even drier. You may think the peanuts sound good enough to eat now. But **raw peanuts,** peanuts that haven't been roasted or boiled, don't taste very good.

Soon the trailers are hooked up to the farmer's trucks. The peanuts aren't going to the peanut butter factory yet, though. First they must go to a peanut buying station to be graded and inspected. Not *all* peanuts are good enough for America's favorite spread.

Trailers are used to dry the peanuts and to carry peanuts to the buying station.

Peanuts are used to make peanut flour, peanut oil, and peanut butter. Plain peanuts are delicious too: oil roasted or dry roasted, with or without skins.

3
Selling, Grading, and Shelling

Near almost every peanut farm, you will find a peanut buying station—an enormous store where businesses buy raw peanuts from farmers.

When the farmers' trucks arrive at the buying station, they stop first at a U.S. government checkpoint. Here an inspector gives each load of peanuts a "report card." The peanuts are graded as either one, two, or three. Grade-one peanuts are the driest, cleanest, and meatiest. These peanuts are the most valuable, and they are the only kind that can be used in human food.

Peanut farmers sell their crops at a buying station.

After the peanuts are graded, they are weighed. The buyers pay the farmers for their crops, and the peanuts are unloaded into a huge pit that holds four to six tons of peanuts. A conveyor belt lifts the peanuts from the pit into a storage tank that looks like a short, fat silo. Within a few days, the raw nuts are loaded into trucks going to the shelling plant.

Outside the shelling plant, the peanuts are dumped into a big pit again. In the pit is an industrial elevator, which doesn't look like the kind of elevator people ride on. It looks like a conveyor belt with pails attached. The pails scoop up the peanuts and flip them onto another conveyor belt, which then carries the peanuts through the plant.

The conveyor belt enters the plant through a large window that's covered by a screen. As the peanuts fall through the screen's holes and into the plant, rocks, leaves, and sticks are left outside.

- There are plenty of uses for grade-two and grade-three peanuts. They are used in making shaving cream, shoe polish, lipstick, and paint. The shells can be used to make insulation and cat litter.

At the shelling plant, peanuts are sorted by size. Only the smallest peanuts will have their shells removed. Large peanuts will be sold in the shell.

Next the conveyor belt carries the peanuts to a machine called a farmer's stock cleaner. This machine is made of a stack of screens that shake back and forth. The farmer's stock cleaner shakes more dirt, tiny stones, and sand from the peanuts.

After the peanuts are cleaned, they are sorted by size. The sorting is done with screens that have special-sized holes. The biggest peanuts remain on top of the screens. These will be roasted in their shells, to be sold as "ballpark peanuts." You've probably eaten peanuts like this at a circus or a baseball game. The smaller peanuts fall through onto a platform below. These smaller peanuts will be **shelled,** which means their shells will be removed. Some of them will be used to make peanut butter.

Now the smaller cleaned peanuts are ready for the shelling machine. A shelling machine is a metal box that's about a foot high and about three feet long. Inside it are rolling baskets called beater baskets. Beater baskets have grates inside them, with holes about the size of peanuts without their shells. The beater baskets also have four metal bars inside, which rotate very fast—about 200 times a minute. The bars push the nuts through the holes in the grates, crushing the shells. The nuts and shells fall through the grate openings, and fans blow the shells away.

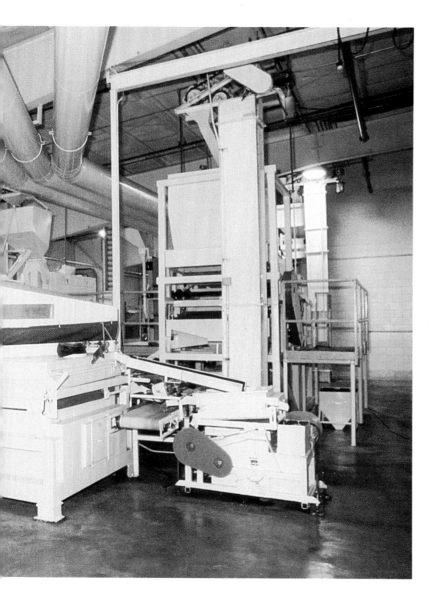

Next the peanuts go into a machine called a gravity separator. It's a strange-looking contraption that's really just a set of metal platforms with fans and boxes underneath. The fans blow any pieces of leftover peanut shells into a cyclone machine—an 18-foot metal cone. The shells are collected and bagged, and later they will be sold. Tiny stones and sand fall to the bottom of the gravity separator and are discarded. The peanuts fall onto a conveyor belt. They are taken from the gravity separator to a room where they will be inspected.

The gravity separator gives the peanuts a final cleaning. It separates the peanuts from any last bits of shells or sand.

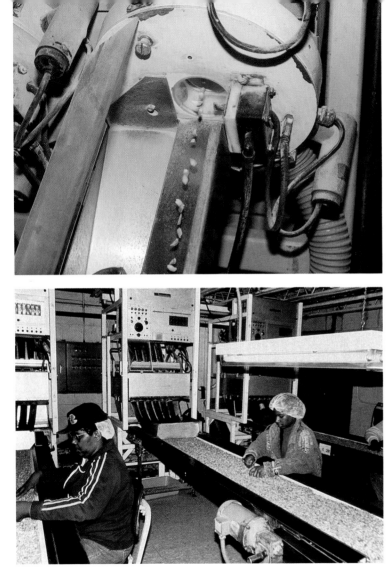

The peanuts are inspected first by electric eyes—beams of light that show workers if any peanuts are unhealthy or discolored. Then workers at a table check the nuts by hand.

Finally, the peanuts are weighed and poured into burlap bags. A worker pushes the bags through a machine that sews the top shut. The bags are thrown down a slide and stacked onto trucks. The peanuts are on their way to the peanut butter factory.

Top: *An electric eye spots dark-colored peanuts.* Bottom: *Factory workers check the peanuts a second time.*

Making the Nutty Spread

When the peanuts arrive at the peanut butter factory, workers remove 50-pound samples of peanuts from each shipment. Then a person called a quality control technician treats the sample peanuts with chemicals in a laboratory. The technician checks the samples for **aflatoxin,** a toxin, or poisonous substance, that is caused by mold in peanuts.

If the peanuts aren't moldy, they go on to be cleaned again. They go through a gravity separator just like the one at the shelling plant. Workers at the peanut butter factories want to be sure that their product is 100 percent clean.

A technician checks peanuts for molds and toxins.

Now the peanuts are roasted. This happens in a large, multi-chamber roasting machine. In the first chamber, the peanuts are cooked at about 350 degrees Fahrenheit. Then they travel on a conveyor belt to the next chamber, where they are cooked again. In the last chambers, they are cooled. This whole process takes about 15 minutes.

- The world's biggest peanut butter cookie weighed in at 150 pounds. It used 26 pounds of peanut butter.

- The world's largest peanut butter factory, located in Ohio, manufactures 250,000 jars of the spread each day.

- The fear of getting peanut butter stuck to the roof of your mouth is Arachibutyrophobia (AHR-uh-kih-BYOO-tih-roh-FOH-bee-uh). Quite a mouthful.

A large roasting oven can cook up to 9,000 pounds of peanuts in an hour.

Next the peanuts are **blanched,** which means that the skins are removed. Peanuts are blanched between two rubber-coated, grooved wheels that look like car tires. As the peanuts pass between them, the wheels loosen the skins. Then a vacuum device sucks the skins off.

Blanched peanuts have had their skins removed.

If they won't be used right away, the blanched peanuts travel to a storage tank. Otherwise, they are piped into a 100-foot-long suction tube called an electronic feed system. The tube sucks the peanuts into a room where they will be ground up.

Peanuts are not the only ingredients that are piped into the feed system. There are three others: vegetable oil, salt, and, if a sweetener is used, sugar or **dextrose.** Dextrose is a powdery sweetener made from corn.

This bag of dextrose weighs 2,000 pounds!

All the ingredients must be piped through the feed system in specific amounts. Let's say that one company's peanut butter recipe is 5 parts dextrose, 3 parts oil, 1 part salt, and 91 parts peanuts. If too much or too little of any ingredient flows into the feed pipe, an alarm goes off. This sound alerts the workers in the peanut butter factory to stop the feed system and check things out.

Computers control the factory's ingredient feed systems. They make sure that a factory's special recipe is followed exactly.

The mixed ingredients are sucked through the feed pipe into a machine called a mill. The mill is made of two metal plates. One plate rotates while the other stays still, and together they grind up the roasted peanuts. The peanuts are now part of a warm, gritty, brown liquid—officially called peanut butter.

Most peanut butter companies do a second grinding to make sure the peanut butter is smooth. Some companies even mix it in a huge mixing bowl that holds up to 2,000 pounds of peanut butter. A giant paddle in the mixing bowl smooths out the peanut butter more.

Mixing is important. A paddle stirs the peanut butter until it's creamy and smooth.

If chunky-style peanut butter is being made, chopped peanuts are poured into the bowl from a hopper. A few companies make their chunky peanut butter in a different way. They just grind the peanut butter once, lightly. This light grinding leaves chunks of peanuts in the peanut butter.

No matter how peanut butter is made, all the mixing and grinding create a lot of air bubbles. Air bubbles make the peanut butter look unappetizing, and they also trap germs. A vacuum pipe sucks the air bubbles from the peanut butter.

The mixing has also made the peanut butter hot—about 140 degrees Fahrenheit. So the peanut butter must be pumped through a cooling system. The cooling system is made of a six-foot pipe within a bigger pipe. As the peanut butter goes through the inner pipe, cold water flows through the outer pipe. The water cools the peanut butter, which helps the vegetable oil "set," or harden.

● You may have eaten "natural" peanut butter, which contains only ground-up peanuts. You need to refrigerate natural peanut butter or stir it before you use it. Do you know why?

Peanuts contain a type of natural oil that becomes a liquid at room temperature. As the oil turns to liquid, it separates from the rest of the peanut butter and floats on top.

Most peanut butter, though, is made with a type of vegetable oil that remains solid at room temperature. The vegetable oil mixes with the peanut oil, and it keeps the peanut butter from separating.

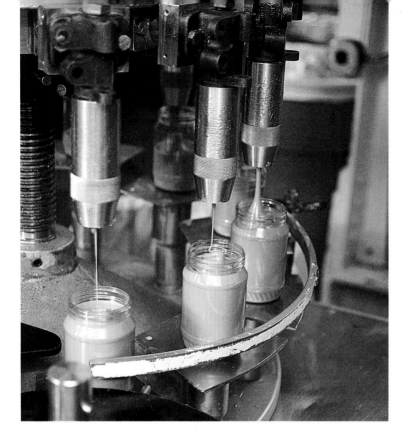

Peanut butter comes out of the filler looking like soft ice cream—the peanut butter inside the jars even has swirls on top. Peanut butter takes 24 to 48 hours to harden into the product you spread on your sandwich.

Next the peanut butter is piped to the factory's filling area and into a machine called a filler. Clean, empty jars move on the conveyor belt toward the filler. As the jars pass beneath the filler's nozzles, the filler squirts peanut butter into the jars. If the peanut butter is going to be the striped-with-jelly kind, another filler squirts jelly into the jars.

Now the jars move down the conveyor belt to be capped. They're packed into boxes and stacked onto wooden frames called pallets. Pallets make it easier for workers to transport boxes around the factory.

A forklift moves the pallets full of boxes to the shipping area. From that point, the peanut butter will be stacked onto trucks. Soon, it will be delivered to the store where you buy peanut butter.

Another machine screws caps on the filled peanut butter jars.

Nutritious and delicious peanut butter—ready to eat!

5
Nutrition in a Nutshell

One of the best things about peanut butter is that it is good for you. Peanuts are often referred to as "nutrition in a nutshell." They contain many **nutrients,** the substances in food that your body needs for good health. Since at least 90 percent of peanut butter is peanuts, it's very nutritious too.

Peanut butter contains the following nutrients: **protein, carbohydrates, fats, vitamins,** and **minerals.** Let's take a look at these nutrients and what they do for you.

Protein

Every cell in your body contains protein. It gives you energy and helps you grow. Two tablespoons of peanut butter offers as much protein as a slice of cheese, a glass of milk, or an egg.

Carbohydrates

Carbohydrates are your body's main source of energy. Peanut butter is so high in carbohydrates that it's considered a high-energy food.

Fats

Fats are another source of energy. Fats work with protein and carbohydrates to help them do their jobs better.

Vitamins and Minerals

Vitamins and minerals are important to your body's growth. They also help other nutrients to do their jobs.

● **Niacin** is a vitamin. It helps break up protein, carbohydrates, and fats to help your body use them. Niacin helps keep your nervous system, mouth, skin, tongue, and digestive tract healthy. Peanut butter and peanuts are some of the richest sources of this vitamin.

- **Riboflavin** is a vitamin that helps keep your vision clear and helps your cells use oxygen. Riboflavin also prevents the skin around your mouth and nose from cracking and scaling.
- **Phosphorus** is a mineral that helps strengthen your teeth and bones. It also helps your body use proteins, carbohydrates, and fat.
- **Magnesium** is a mineral that helps regulate your body temperature. Magnesium helps build your bones, the enamel on your teeth, and body tissues. It also helps your body absorb other nutrients.
- **Iron** is a very important mineral. It combines with protein to make the red substance in your blood called hemoglobin. Hemoglobin carries oxygen to all your cells.

Your body needs every one of these important nutrients, and peanut butter provides them for you. When you have peanut butter with fruits or vegetables and milk, you are eating a balanced meal.

Make Your Own Peanut Butter

Most people buy peanut butter at the supermarket, but it's easy to make it at home. Your homemade peanut butter won't look or taste exactly like supermarket peanut butter. It will still taste good, though.

HOMEMADE PEANUT BUTTER

Ingredients:

1 cup shelled peanuts
1 and 1/2 tablespoons peanut oil
1/2 teaspoon salt

Equipment:

Blender or food processor
Measuring spoons
Measuring cup
Rubber spatula
A small jar or plastic container, with a lid

Put the peanuts into the blender or food processor. Blend for about one minute, until peanuts are finely crushed into a paste. Stir in the oil and salt.

Try the peanut butter on a cracker or celery stalk. Yummy, isn't it?

Put your homemade peanut butter into a covered container. This peanut butter needs to be refrigerated. Also, the oil will probably separate from the peanuts. Don't worry about that—you just need to stir the peanut butter before you eat it again.

UNUSUAL NUTTY BUTTERS

Here are ways to make your peanut butter taste even better:

Honey Peanut Butter

Pour 1/4 cup of honey into the nuts after grinding them. Then blend the nuts again for a few seconds.

Raisin Peanut Butter

After your peanut butter is done, stir in 1/2 cup of raisins with a spoon. (Don't add the raisins in the blender or they will get smashed.)

Cinnamon Peanut Butter

Stir a teaspoon of cinnamon into your peanut butter. This tastes great.

Super Crunchy Peanut Butter

Add 1/4 cup of chopped peanuts to the mixture. You can chop these in the blender before you make the peanut butter. Remember to chop them for only about five seconds and remove them before you crush the rest of the peanuts. Blend them into your finished peanut butter with a wooden spoon or rubber spatula.

PEANUT BUTTER ORANGE SANDWICH

Ingredients:

2 tablespoons peanut butter
2 teaspoons orange juice
1 teaspoon grated orange peel
2 slices bread

Equipment:

Measuring spoons
Small bowl
Grater
Juice squeezer

In a bowl, thoroughly mix peanut butter, juice, and orange peel. Spread on one slice of bread. Cover with the remaining slice. Makes one sandwich.

PEANUT BUTTER RAISIN DELIGHT

Ingredients:

2 tablespoons peanut butter
2 tablespoons raisins
2 slices bread
2 tablespoons grated carrot

Equipment:

Measuring spoons
Small bowl
Grater
Spoon
Table knife

In a bowl, mix peanut butter with raisins. Spread mixture on one slice of bread. Sprinkle with grated carrot and cover with the other slice of bread. Makes one sandwich.

PEANUT BUTTER CRUNCH BALLS

Ingredients:

1/2 cup peanut butter
1/2 cup honey
1 cup dry milk
1 cup chopped peanuts

Equipment:

Measuring cups
2 small bowls
Wooden spoon
Plate

Mix peanut butter and honey in a bowl. Add dry milk a little at a time to make a claylike mixture. With your hands, form the mixture into balls about the size of a nickel. Roll the balls in chopped peanuts and serve. Makes about 1 to 1 and 1/2 dozen.

ANTS ON A LOG

Ingredients:

Celery stalks, cut into 6-inch pieces
Smooth peanut butter
Raisins

Equipment:

Table knife

Fill the groove in each piece of celery with a tablespoon of peanut butter. Dot with raisins.

PEANUT BUTTER APPLE SANDWICH

Ingredients:

1 small apple
1/4 cup peanut butter
1/4 teaspoon lemon juice
4 slices bread

Equipment:

Measuring spoons
Grater
Small bowl
Table knife
Small sharp knife

Cut apple in half and remove seeds and stem. Grate apple, including the peel. (This makes a pretty spread.) In a small bowl, mix the grated apple with peanut butter and lemon juice. Spread the mixture on two slices of bread. Top sandwiches with remaining bread. Makes two sandwiches.

PEANUT BUTTER BANANA SHAKE

Ingredients:

1 banana
1/4 cup smooth peanut butter
1 cup milk
1/2 pint vanilla ice cream

Equipment:

Blender
Dry measuring cups
Liquid measuring cups
Small sharp knife
Tall glasses

Peel banana and slice. Put into blender with peanut butter. Blend until smooth. Add milk and ice cream. Blend until nice and frothy. Serve in tall glasses. Makes two shakes.

METRIC CONVERSION CHART

WHEN YOU KNOW:	MULTIPLY BY:	TO FIND:
AREA		
acres	.41	hectares
LENGTH		
inches	25.00	millimeters
inches	2.54	centimeters
feet	30.00	centimeters
feet	.30	meters
yards	.91	meters
miles	1.61	kilometers
VOLUME		
teaspoons	5.00	milliliters
tablespoons	15.00	milliliters
fluid ounces	30.00	milliliters
cups	0.24	liters
pints	0.47	liters
quarts	0.95	liters
gallons	3.80	liters
WEIGHT		
ounces	28.00	grams
pounds	0.45	kilograms
tons	0.91	metric tons
TEMPERATURE		
Fahrenheit temperature	5/9 (after subtracting 32)	Celsius temperature

FREE PEANUT BUTTER STUFF

You can receive a free comic book about peanuts and peanut butter when you write to this address:

Director of Consumer Foods and Services
Georgia Peanut Commission
Box 967
Tifton, GA 31793

The Georgia Peanut Commission also sponsors the Adults Only Peanut Butter Lovers' Fan Club. It costs $3.00 a year for a button, membership card, and newsletter four times a year. Even though they call it an "adults only" club, they do take kids for members. You can write the club at the address above.

GLOSSARY

aflatoxin: a toxic (poisonous) substance that is produced by mold in peanuts or other crops

blanched peanuts: peanuts that have had their skins removed

carbohydrates: nutrients that supply the body with energy and are found in the starches and sugars of food

dextrose: a type of sugar found in plants and animals; also called glucose

fats: nutrients that supply the body with energy. Fats are oily or greasy substances found in animals and in plant seeds.

minerals: certain elements needed by plants and animals for growth and the maintenance of body structures

nutrients: the many different substances in food that the body needs for good health

protein: a substance found in the cells of all living things. Protein is an important nutrient that gives the body energy and helps it grow.

raw peanuts: peanuts that have not been roasted or boiled

shelled peanuts: peanuts that have had their shells removed

vitamins: substances needed by the body in very small amounts to keep healthy

INDEX

ACKNOWLEDGMENTS

This book would not have been possible without the generous help of the following people and organizations:

Ms. Sherry Lightsey, Distribution Manager, Georgia Peanut Commission; Mr. W. J. Spain, Chief Executive Officer, Birdsong Peanut Company; Mr. Jerry Needham, Production Manager, John B. San Filippo & Son, Inc.; Mike Valentine, General Manager, John B. San Filippo & Son, Inc.; Mr. Eddie Crosby, Carter Manufacturing Company; Lewis M. Carter Manufacturing; Mitch Head, Executive Director, Peanut Advisory Board.

The publisher would like to thank Natalie Lund, John Murphy, Joseph Murphy, Ted Seykora, and Ty Thompson.

ABOUT THE AUTHOR

Arlene Erlbach has written more than a dozen books of fiction and nonfiction for young people. In addition to being an author, she is an elementary school teacher. She loves to encourage children to read and write, and she is in charge of her school's Young Authors' program. Ms. Erlbach lives in Morton Grove, Illinois, with her husband, her son, a collie, and three cats.